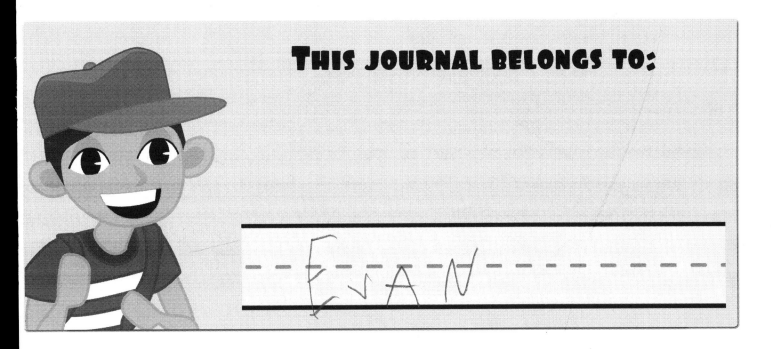

THIS JOURNAL BELONGS TO:

EVAN

BigRedBalloonBooks.com

Cover and page design by Big Red Balloon Studios - Copyright 2013

ISBN-13: 978-1494376857
ISBN-10: 1494376857

DRAW A PICTURE OF TODAY'S DISCOVERY

SHARE WHAT YOU SEE, SMELL, HEAR, OR FEEL.

DRAW A PICTURE OF TODAY'S DISCOVERY

SHARE WHAT YOU SEE, SMELL, HEAR, OR FEEL.

DRAW A PICTURE OF TODAY'S DISCOVERY

SHARE WHAT YOU SEE, SMELL, HEAR, OR FEEL.

DRAW A PICTURE OF TODAY'S DISCOVERY

SHARE WHAT YOU SEE, SMELL, HEAR, OR FEEL.

DRAW A PICTURE OF TODAY'S DISCOVERY

SHARE WHAT YOU SEE, SMELL, HEAR, OR FEEL.

DRAW A PICTURE OF TODAY'S DISCOVERY

SHARE WHAT YOU SEE, SMELL, HEAR, OR FEEL.

DRAW A PICTURE OF TODAY'S DISCOVERY

SHARE WHAT YOU SEE, SMELL, HEAR, OR FEEL.

DRAW A PICTURE OF TODAY'S DISCOVERY

SHARE WHAT YOU SEE, SMELL, HEAR, OR FEEL.

DRAW A PICTURE OF TODAY'S DISCOVERY

SHARE WHAT YOU SEE, SMELL, HEAR, OR FEEL.

DRAW A PICTURE OF TODAY'S DISCOVERY

SHARE WHAT YOU SEE, SMELL, HEAR, OR FEEL.

DRAW A PICTURE OF TODAY'S DISCOVERY

SHARE WHAT YOU SEE, SMELL, HEAR, OR FEEL.

DRAW A PICTURE OF TODAY'S DISCOVERY

SHARE WHAT YOU SEE, SMELL, HEAR, OR FEEL.

DRAW A PICTURE OF TODAY'S DISCOVERY

SHARE WHAT YOU SEE, SMELL, HEAR, OR FEEL.

DRAW A PICTURE OF TODAY'S DISCOVERY

SHARE WHAT YOU SEE, SMELL, HEAR, OR FEEL.

DRAW A PICTURE OF TODAY'S DISCOVERY

SHARE WHAT YOU SEE, SMELL, HEAR, OR FEEL.

DRAW A PICTURE OF TODAY'S DISCOVERY

SHARE WHAT YOU SEE, SMELL, HEAR, OR FEEL.

DRAW A PICTURE OF TODAY'S DISCOVERY

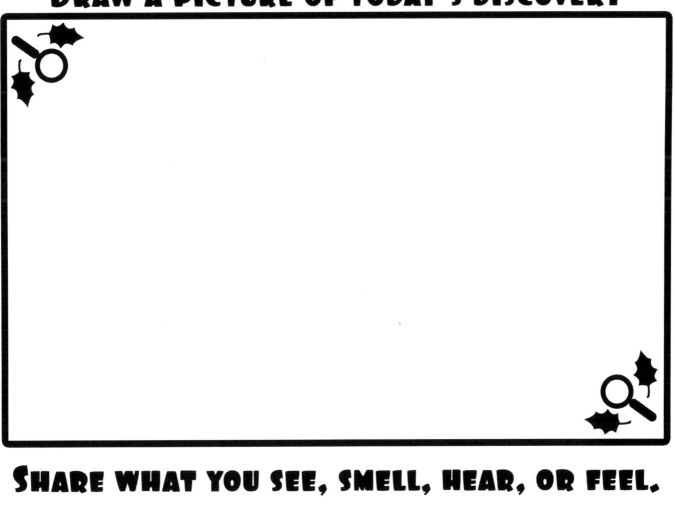

SHARE WHAT YOU SEE, SMELL, HEAR, OR FEEL.

DRAW A PICTURE OF TODAY'S DISCOVERY

SHARE WHAT YOU SEE, SMELL, HEAR, OR FEEL.

DRAW A PICTURE OF TODAY'S DISCOVERY

SHARE WHAT YOU SEE, SMELL, HEAR, OR FEEL.

DRAW A PICTURE OF TODAY'S DISCOVERY

SHARE WHAT YOU SEE, SMELL, HEAR, OR FEEL.

DRAW A PICTURE OF TODAY'S DISCOVERY

SHARE WHAT YOU SEE, SMELL, HEAR, OR FEEL.

DRAW A PICTURE OF TODAY'S DISCOVERY

SHARE WHAT YOU SEE, SMELL, HEAR, OR FEEL.

DRAW A PICTURE OF TODAY'S DISCOVERY

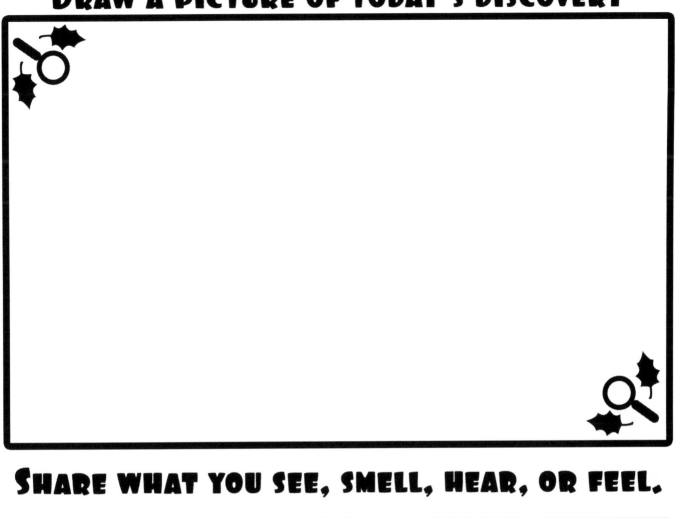

SHARE WHAT YOU SEE, SMELL, HEAR, OR FEEL.

DRAW A PICTURE OF TODAY'S DISCOVERY

SHARE WHAT YOU SEE, SMELL, HEAR, OR FEEL.

DRAW A PICTURE OF TODAY'S DISCOVERY

SHARE WHAT YOU SEE, SMELL, HEAR, OR FEEL.

DRAW A PICTURE OF TODAY'S DISCOVERY

SHARE WHAT YOU SEE, SMELL, HEAR, OR FEEL.

DRAW A PICTURE OF TODAY'S DISCOVERY

SHARE WHAT YOU SEE, SMELL, HEAR, OR FEEL.

DRAW A PICTURE OF TODAY'S DISCOVERY

SHARE WHAT YOU SEE, SMELL, HEAR, OR FEEL.

DRAW A PICTURE OF TODAY'S DISCOVERY

SHARE WHAT YOU SEE, SMELL, HEAR, OR FEEL.

DRAW A PICTURE OF TODAY'S DISCOVERY

SHARE WHAT YOU SEE, SMELL, HEAR, OR FEEL.

DRAW A PICTURE OF TODAY'S DISCOVERY

SHARE WHAT YOU SEE, SMELL, HEAR, OR FEEL.

DRAW A PICTURE OF TODAY'S DISCOVERY

SHARE WHAT YOU SEE, SMELL, HEAR, OR FEEL.

DRAW A PICTURE OF TODAY'S DISCOVERY

SHARE WHAT YOU SEE, SMELL, HEAR, OR FEEL.

DRAW A PICTURE OF TODAY'S DISCOVERY

SHARE WHAT YOU SEE, SMELL, HEAR, OR FEEL.

DRAW A PICTURE OF TODAY'S DISCOVERY

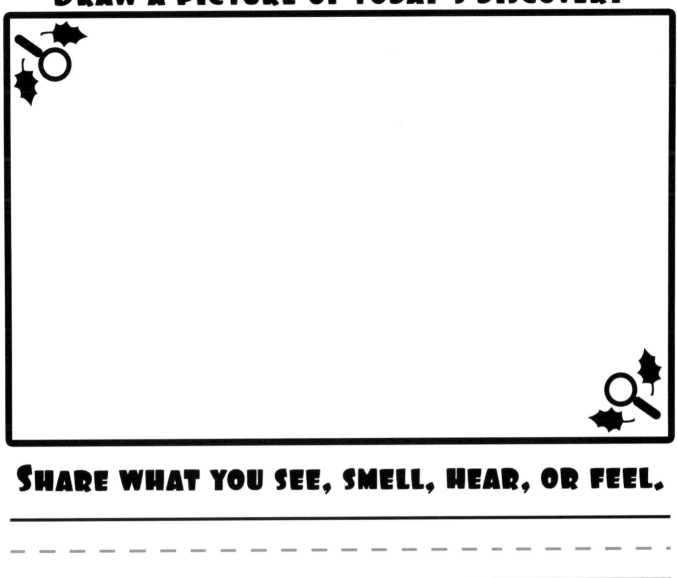

SHARE WHAT YOU SEE, SMELL, HEAR, OR FEEL.

DRAW A PICTURE OF TODAY'S DISCOVERY

SHARE WHAT YOU SEE, SMELL, HEAR, OR FEEL.

DRAW A PICTURE OF TODAY'S DISCOVERY

SHARE WHAT YOU SEE, SMELL, HEAR, OR FEEL.

DRAW A PICTURE OF TODAY'S DISCOVERY

SHARE WHAT YOU SEE, SMELL, HEAR, OR FEEL.

DRAW A PICTURE OF TODAY'S DISCOVERY

SHARE WHAT YOU SEE, SMELL, HEAR, OR FEEL.

DRAW A PICTURE OF TODAY'S DISCOVERY

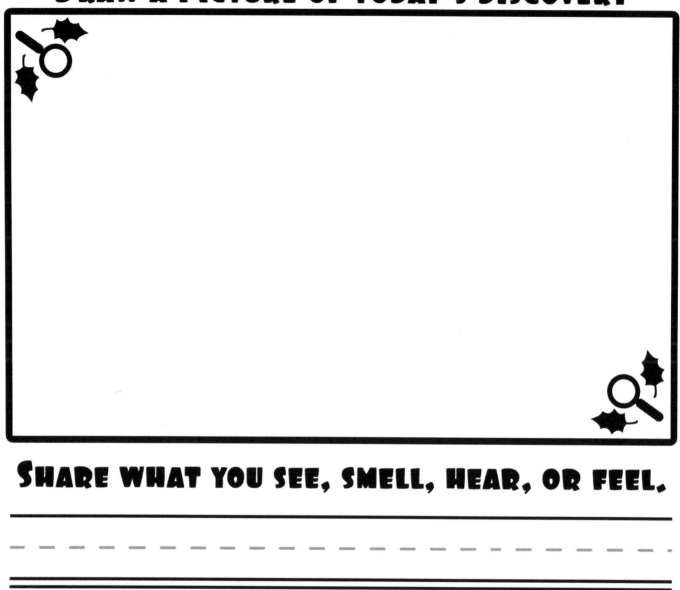

SHARE WHAT YOU SEE, SMELL, HEAR, OR FEEL.

DRAW A PICTURE OF TODAY'S DISCOVERY

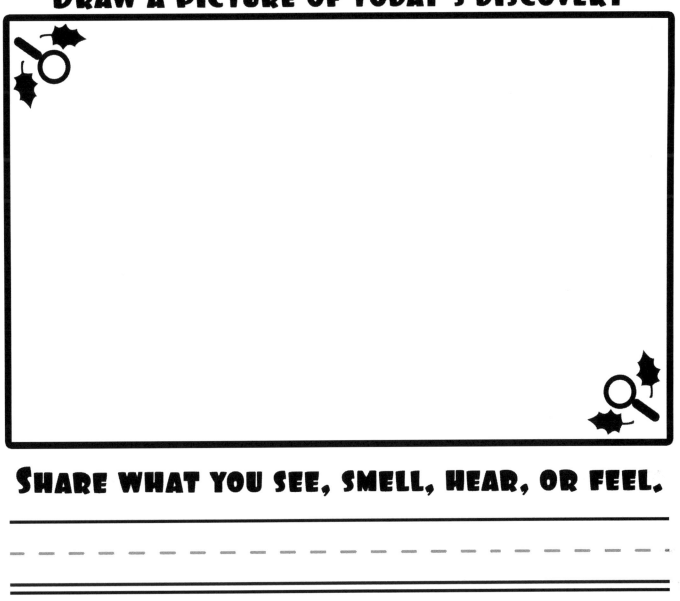

SHARE WHAT YOU SEE, SMELL, HEAR, OR FEEL.

DRAW A PICTURE OF TODAY'S DISCOVERY

SHARE WHAT YOU SEE, SMELL, HEAR, OR FEEL.

DRAW A PICTURE OF TODAY'S DISCOVERY

SHARE WHAT YOU SEE, SMELL, HEAR, OR FEEL.

DRAW A PICTURE OF TODAY'S DISCOVERY

SHARE WHAT YOU SEE, SMELL, HEAR, OR FEEL.

DRAW A PICTURE OF TODAY'S DISCOVERY

SHARE WHAT YOU SEE, SMELL, HEAR, OR FEEL.

DRAW A PICTURE OF TODAY'S DISCOVERY

SHARE WHAT YOU SEE, SMELL, HEAR, OR FEEL.

DRAW A PICTURE OF TODAY'S DISCOVERY

SHARE WHAT YOU SEE, SMELL, HEAR, OR FEEL.

DRAW A PICTURE OF TODAY'S DISCOVERY

SHARE WHAT YOU SEE, SMELL, HEAR, OR FEEL.

DRAW A PICTURE OF TODAY'S DISCOVERY

SHARE WHAT YOU SEE, SMELL, HEAR, OR FEEL.

DRAW A PICTURE OF TODAY'S DISCOVERY

SHARE WHAT YOU SEE, SMELL, HEAR, OR FEEL.

DRAW A PICTURE OF TODAY'S DISCOVERY

SHARE WHAT YOU SEE, SMELL, HEAR, OR FEEL.

DRAW A PICTURE OF TODAY'S DISCOVERY

SHARE WHAT YOU SEE, SMELL, HEAR, OR FEEL.

DRAW A PICTURE OF TODAY'S DISCOVERY

SHARE WHAT YOU SEE, SMELL, HEAR, OR FEEL.

DRAW A PICTURE OF TODAY'S DISCOVERY

SHARE WHAT YOU SEE, SMELL, HEAR, OR FEEL.

DRAW A PICTURE OF TODAY'S DISCOVERY

SHARE WHAT YOU SEE, SMELL, HEAR, OR FEEL.

DRAW A PICTURE OF TODAY'S DISCOVERY

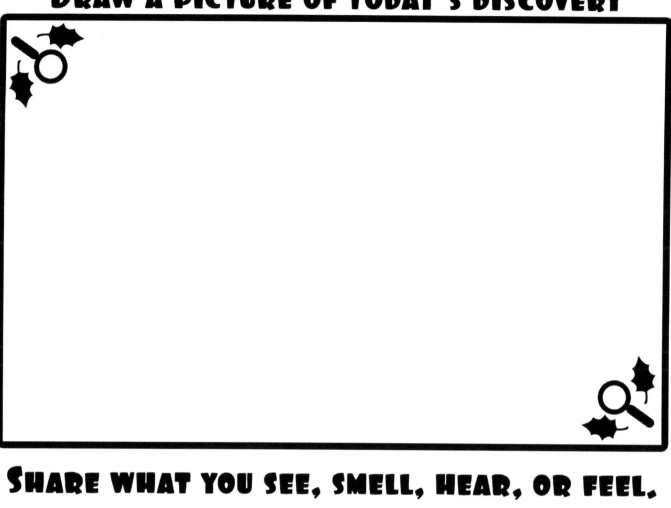

SHARE WHAT YOU SEE, SMELL, HEAR, OR FEEL.

DRAW A PICTURE OF TODAY'S DISCOVERY

SHARE WHAT YOU SEE, SMELL, HEAR, OR FEEL.

DRAW A PICTURE OF TODAY'S DISCOVERY

SHARE WHAT YOU SEE, SMELL, HEAR, OR FEEL.

DRAW A PICTURE OF TODAY'S DISCOVERY

SHARE WHAT YOU SEE, SMELL, HEAR, OR FEEL.

DRAW A PICTURE OF TODAY'S DISCOVERY

SHARE WHAT YOU SEE, SMELL, HEAR, OR FEEL.

DRAW A PICTURE OF TODAY'S DISCOVERY

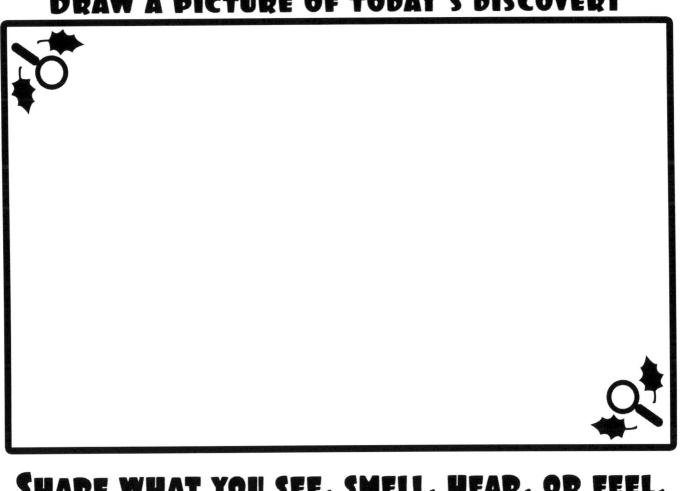

SHARE WHAT YOU SEE, SMELL, HEAR, OR FEEL.

DRAW A PICTURE OF TODAY'S DISCOVERY

SHARE WHAT YOU SEE, SMELL, HEAR, OR FEEL.

DRAW A PICTURE OF TODAY'S DISCOVERY

SHARE WHAT YOU SEE, SMELL, HEAR, OR FEEL.

DRAW A PICTURE OF TODAY'S DISCOVERY

SHARE WHAT YOU SEE, SMELL, HEAR, OR FEEL.

DRAW A PICTURE OF TODAY'S DISCOVERY

SHARE WHAT YOU SEE, SMELL, HEAR, OR FEEL.

DRAW A PICTURE OF TODAY'S DISCOVERY

SHARE WHAT YOU SEE, SMELL, HEAR, OR FEEL.

DRAW A PICTURE OF TODAY'S DISCOVERY

SHARE WHAT YOU SEE, SMELL, HEAR, OR FEEL.

DRAW A PICTURE OF TODAY'S DISCOVERY

SHARE WHAT YOU SEE, SMELL, HEAR, OR FEEL.

DRAW A PICTURE OF TODAY'S DISCOVERY

SHARE WHAT YOU SEE, SMELL, HEAR, OR FEEL.

DRAW A PICTURE OF TODAY'S DISCOVERY

SHARE WHAT YOU SEE, SMELL, HEAR, OR FEEL.

DRAW A PICTURE OF TODAY'S DISCOVERY

SHARE WHAT YOU SEE, SMELL, HEAR, OR FEEL.

DRAW A PICTURE OF TODAY'S DISCOVERY

SHARE WHAT YOU SEE, SMELL, HEAR, OR FEEL.

DRAW A PICTURE OF TODAY'S DISCOVERY

SHARE WHAT YOU SEE, SMELL, HEAR, OR FEEL.

DRAW A PICTURE OF TODAY'S DISCOVERY

SHARE WHAT YOU SEE, SMELL, HEAR, OR FEEL.

DRAW A PICTURE OF TODAY'S DISCOVERY

SHARE WHAT YOU SEE, SMELL, HEAR, OR FEEL.

DRAW A PICTURE OF TODAY'S DISCOVERY

SHARE WHAT YOU SEE, SMELL, HEAR, OR FEEL.

DRAW A PICTURE OF TODAY'S DISCOVERY

SHARE WHAT YOU SEE, SMELL, HEAR, OR FEEL.

DRAW A PICTURE OF TODAY'S DISCOVERY

SHARE WHAT YOU SEE, SMELL, HEAR, OR FEEL.

DRAW A PICTURE OF TODAY'S DISCOVERY

SHARE WHAT YOU SEE, SMELL, HEAR, OR FEEL.

DRAW A PICTURE OF TODAY'S DISCOVERY

SHARE WHAT YOU SEE, SMELL, HEAR, OR FEEL.

DRAW A PICTURE OF TODAY'S DISCOVERY

SHARE WHAT YOU SEE, SMELL, HEAR, OR FEEL.

DRAW A PICTURE OF TODAY'S DISCOVERY

SHARE WHAT YOU SEE, SMELL, HEAR, OR FEEL.

DRAW A PICTURE OF TODAY'S DISCOVERY

SHARE WHAT YOU SEE, SMELL, HEAR, OR FEEL.

DRAW A PICTURE OF TODAY'S DISCOVERY

SHARE WHAT YOU SEE, SMELL, HEAR, OR FEEL.

DRAW A PICTURE OF TODAY'S DISCOVERY

SHARE WHAT YOU SEE, SMELL, HEAR, OR FEEL.

DRAW A PICTURE OF TODAY'S DISCOVERY

SHARE WHAT YOU SEE, SMELL, HEAR, OR FEEL.

DRAW A PICTURE OF TODAY'S DISCOVERY

SHARE WHAT YOU SEE, SMELL, HEAR, OR FEEL.

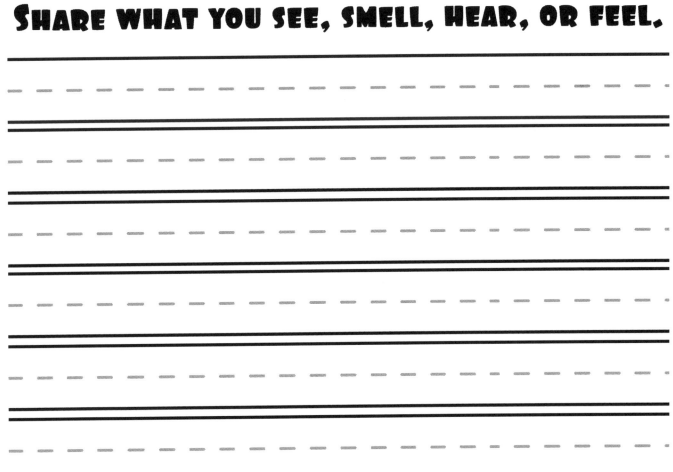

DRAW A PICTURE OF TODAY'S DISCOVERY

SHARE WHAT YOU SEE, SMELL, HEAR, OR FEEL.

DRAW A PICTURE OF TODAY'S DISCOVERY

SHARE WHAT YOU SEE, SMELL, HEAR, OR FEEL.

DRAW A PICTURE OF TODAY'S DISCOVERY

SHARE WHAT YOU SEE, SMELL, HEAR, OR FEEL.

DRAW A PICTURE OF TODAY'S DISCOVERY

SHARE WHAT YOU SEE, SMELL, HEAR, OR FEEL.

DRAW A PICTURE OF TODAY'S DISCOVERY

SHARE WHAT YOU SEE, SMELL, HEAR, OR FEEL.

DRAW A PICTURE OF TODAY'S DISCOVERY

SHARE WHAT YOU SEE, SMELL, HEAR, OR FEEL.

DRAW A PICTURE OF TODAY'S DISCOVERY

SHARE WHAT YOU SEE, SMELL, HEAR, OR FEEL.

DRAW A PICTURE OF TODAY'S DISCOVERY

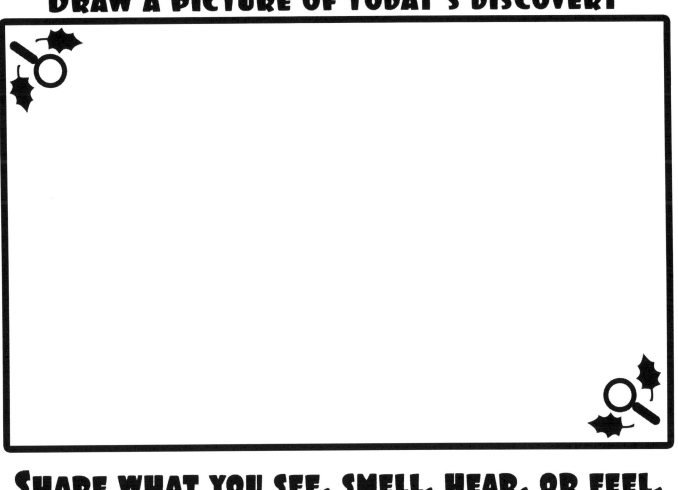

SHARE WHAT YOU SEE, SMELL, HEAR, OR FEEL.

Made in the USA
San Bernardino, CA
24 June 2015